ENCOUNTERS
WITH JESUS

21 DAYS OF DRAWING CLOSE
TO THE SON

CJ Hitz

Encounters with Jesus: 21 Days of Drawing Close to the Son
By CJ Hitz
Published by Body and Soul Publishing LLC
Colorado Springs, CO 80904
© 2020 CJ Hitz

Edited by Deb Hall, (http://thewriteinsight.com)
ISBN 978-1-946118-17-2

Day 12 "How Bad Do You Want It" used with permission by Dr. Gwen Ebner

Unless otherwise indicated, all Scripture quotations are taken from the Holy Bible, New Living Translation, copyright © 1996, 2004, 2007, 2013 by Tyndale House Foundation. Used by permission of Tyndale House Publishers, Inc., Carol Stream, Illinois 60188. All rights reserved.

Scripture quotations marked (MSG) taken from The Message. Copyright © by Eugene H. Peterson 1993, 1994, 1995, 1996, 2000, 2001, 2002. Used by permission of Tyndale House Publishers, Inc.

Scripture quotations marked (NIV) are taken from the Holy Bible, New International Version®, NIV®. Copyright © 1973, 1978, 1984, 2011 by Biblica, Inc.™ Used by permission of Zondervan. All rights reserved worldwide. www.zondervan.com The "NIV" and "New International Version" are trademarks registered in the United States Patent and Trademark Office by Biblica, Inc.™

Scripture marked (NKJV) taken from the New King James Version®. Copyright © 1982 by Thomas Nelson. Used by permission. All rights reserved.

CONTENTS

INTRODUCTION

When we "encounter" something, we are coming face-to-face with it. More specifically, Merriam-Webster says, to encounter is "to come upon or experience especially unexpectedly."

Whether it was Paul on the road to Damascus, the Samaritan woman at the well, or the demon-possessed man on the shores of Galilee, those who encountered Jesus were changed in unexpected ways.

As we read through the four gospel accounts, there were certainly many who followed Jesus from a distance. Some were amazed by his miracles while others were offended by his teachings. What we find very little of is neutrality or indifference. People either loved or hated this carpenter's son who hailed from Nazareth.

In Luke 24, we see an interesting encounter between the resurrected Jesus and two of his followers as they were walking from Jerusalem to the town of Emmaus. Luke tells us that "Jesus himself suddenly came and began walking with them" (Luke 24:15).

And then in verse 16 we read, "But God kept them from recognizing him."

For the next several miles, the Son of God in disguise proceeds to give the troubled travelers a Bible lesson reminding them of all that the Scriptures had predicted concerning the Messiah.

Whatever Jesus shared with them on the journey was enough to whet the appetites of this pair. They wanted to hear more from their new mystery friend, so they invited him to crash at their place for the night.

Sitting at the dinner table, Jesus took some bread and blessed it before breaking it and giving it to the oblivious hosts. And then it happened:

"Suddenly, their eyes were opened, and they recognized him. And at that moment he disappeared!" (Luke 24:31).

Poof! Gone in sixty-hundredths of a second. I can almost visualize Jesus, twinkle in his eye, flashing a knowing grin just prior to his exit. It was all they needed to be filled with hope.

With the freshly broken bread still in their hands, they asked, "Didn't our hearts burn within us as he talked with us on the road and explained the Scriptures to us?" (Luke 24:32).

It's my hope that over these next twenty-one days, we'll notice our own hearts burning within us as we walk with Jesus. Perhaps we'll find ourselves having a deeper desire to draw closer to the Son as we encounter Him in unexpected ways.

DAY 1
Family History

Read: Matthew 1:1–17

With advancements in technology, it seems that researching family background has become a big business. Ancestry.com alone reports having over 3 million paying subscribers, 15 million DNA tests, and over $1 billion revenue in 2017. This same company has 20 billion records representing 80 countries of origin, 100 million family trees, and 13 billion connections. Whew! Don't worry, I'm sure you can find Great-Great-Great-Great-Grandpa in there.

The Bible is no stranger to genealogies. But be honest, do you find yourself rushing through these long sections of family history or even skipping them altogether? If you're reading the King James Version, that's a lot of "begats" to wade through.

Recently, I began reading the Gospel of Matthew and seriously contemplated blowing over the first seventeen verses of chapter 1. This section is referred to as the "The Ancestors of Jesus the Messiah." As I reluctantly began to read through the lineage of Jesus, I found myself pausing on verses 5–6:

Salmon was the father of Boaz (whose mother was Rahab).

Boaz was the father of Obed (whose mother was Ruth).

Obed was the father of Jesse.

Huh. In all my previous readings of this section, I somehow overlooked the fact that Boaz's mom was Rahab. Yes, Rahab the prostitute. The same Rahab who helped the spies in Joshua 2. As a result, Rahab and her family were the only ones spared when Jericho was destroyed in Joshua 6.

"So Joshua spared Rahab the prostitute and her relatives who were with her in the house, because she had hidden the spies Joshua sent to Jericho. And she lives among the Israelites to this day" (Joshua 6:25).

I wonder if Boaz's father, Salmon, was one of those two spies? (Maybe Ancestry.com could tell us.) Regardless, this Israelite man made the decision to marry a foreigner who had previously earned her living by sleeping around.

Rahab would then give birth to Boaz, who would eventually marry another foreigner named Ruth (a Moabite widow). Could it be that Boaz had a soft spot in his heart for foreigners in light of his mother's background?

Somehow Rahab and Ruth find themselves listed in the Who's Who of Jesus's family tree. There's no attempt at a cover-up. No dirty little secret to hide. Instead, we see the grace of God on full display. This tree of grace eventually bears the fruit of Jesus the Messiah.

And then there's you and me. Once enemies of God. Once foreign to his ways. We now find ourselves the recipients of extravagant grace paid in full with the blood of the royal Son. We can now point to a Roman cross on top of Golgotha when asked about our "family tree."

The rest is history.

Reflection: How does knowing the genealogy of Jesus impact the way you see your own family history?

DAY 2
From Death to Life

Read: John 8:1–11

There she stood trembling, half naked in front of a gawking crowd. This woman had somehow been caught in the act of adultery and was now on death row. No word of the mystery man involved, but it does "take two to tango," as the saying goes.

Regardless, the local "law enforcers" were delighted at the prospect of using the adulteress to trap the man from Nazareth who just happened to be in town (how convenient).

"'What do you think, Teacher? Moses told us she deserves the death penalty'"—they were referring to Leviticus 20:10—"'but what do you say?' they sneered." (John 8:4–5).

I can only imagine the deafening silence that hung in the air as everyone, including a terrified woman, waited for the Rabbi's response as he stooped down to write in the dirt. Finally, Jesus uttered words that have silenced religious types for centuries ever since: "Let the one who has never sinned throw the first stone!" (John 8:7).

One by one, the enforcers took their toys and went home. When the dust had settled, only Jesus and the woman were left. Likewise, for me, at the end of the day—or at the end of my life—the only person coming to my own defense will be Jesus.

This same Jesus took adultery to another level when he said, "Anyone who even looks at a woman with lust has already committed adultery with her in his heart" (Matthew 5:28).

In that case, I'm a dead man walking. I remember how dirty I felt on January 10, 1998. That was the day I stumbled upon internet porn. I would proceed to fall into this mudhole on numerous occasions, including many years into my marriage. It was my "dirty little secret" that nobody, including my loving wife, needed to know about.

The longer I kept these sins in the dark, the more my shame accumulated like mold in a damp basement void of light. This shame affected every other area of my life, whether others could see it or not.

Freedom and healing would eventually come after confessing my sin, as James 5:16 encourages us to do. Just as mold begins to die when exposed to sunlight, sin's hold on me began to die when exposed to the Son's Light.

This woman's accusers had no idea that exposing her sin in the presence of Jesus would ultimately backfire on them. They went from being trappers to being trapped and from executioners to excused.

While these religious elites were preparing to write the ending of this woman's life with stones of all shapes and sizes, the Teacher was busy doing some writing of his own.

Though we don't know the exact words he scribbled in the dust that day, it's safe to say that the Author of life wrote the beginning of a new chapter for the woman standing before him.

I'm thankful my accusers don't have the last word.

At the end of my life, it's just me and Jesus.

Reflection: What do you need to bring before Jesus today in order to experience his complete forgiveness and release from shame?

DAY 3
The Mathematics of Jesus

Read: Matthew 20:1–16

No fair! Not in our eyes anyway. Jesus tells this story about an owner of an estate who hires some people to work in his vineyard. Some of these workers show up at the crack of dawn, some show midmorning, some at lunch time, another group midafternoon, and then one more batch shows up one hour before closing time.

At the end of the day, when paychecks are being handed out, folks start noticing each check is exactly the same, regardless of how many hours each person worked. Before long, the grumbling begins, and one worker slowly approaches the owner. I imagine it went something like this,

WORKER. Uh, boss?

OWNER. Yes?

WORKER. The boys and I have been talking, and it seems you made a mistake with the paychecks.

OWNER. Oh?

WORKER. Yeah, those slackers who showed up an hour before quittin' time got the same amount as those of us who broke our backs the whole day in that scorching heat!

OWNER. So?

WORKER. So . . . it ain't fair!!

OWNER. What do you mean it ain't fair? Didn't I pay you the wage you agreed to?

WORKER. Well . . . yeah, but . . .

OWNER. No buts about it! I've got every right in the universe to pay my workers what I want, regardless of the time they clock in.

*Note: I sometimes imagine the "worker" having a thick New York accent like Paulie in the movie Rocky.

The passage continues, "And so it is, Jesus said, that many who are first now will be last then; and those who are last now will be first then" (Matthew 20:16).

This is no doubt some crazy calculating, huh? What are we to conclude after reading a story like this? Some may call this communism, though I doubt there's a communist country anywhere in the world that would pay the "one-hour slackers" the same as those who'd worked all day.

Some may say this kind of system would create a regular practice of folks showing up an hour before quittin' time, thinking they'd get the same wage. Do you really think an owner like this could be taken advantage of repeatedly like this? Don't think so. There's a theme in this story that I think can be summed up in a word: grace.

A good definition for grace would be getting something good that we don't deserve. Imagine an atmosphere where folks showed up for work knowing the boss just might bless them with something unexpected or even undeserved. Now translate that same formula in life.

Imagine serving a God who just loves blessing the socks off folks who don't always deserve it. A God who gives the same reward (eternal life) to someone putting their trust in him at eight years old as he gives to the person who's eighty-four before making the same decision.

A God who treats the high school dropout the same as the doctor. A God who extends the same love to both the disabled person and the most talented athlete. Some might call this a "waste" of good resources, and they would be correct. Divine grace does have a wastefulness about it. That's the nature of this Jesus and his Father. God simply loves to waste—or shower, you could say—his vast resources on those of us who've spit in his face at one point or another in our lives.

This kind of arithmetic, to our human minds, will never seem to add up. If we would begin leaving the calculations to God rather than playing the "that's not fair" game, we would find ourselves grateful for what we've each been given, not focused on anyone else.

Reflection: How does this crazy story Jesus told impact the way you look at grace? Which of the workers in the story do you find yourself identifying with the most, and why?

DAY 4
Jesus and Tonka Trucks

Read: John 1:1–18

Recently we've had some construction going on behind the condo complex where we live. It's fun to watch these Cat tractors doing their thing as they rearrange the earth. Grown adults playing in the dirt . . . .and getting paid for it! This reminded me of my love for Tonka trucks as a young boy.

I have fond memories of visiting my grandparents in Byron, Wyoming, when I was growing up. Our family would load up the car and make the twenty-two-hour drive from Myrtle Creek, Oregon, over the course of two to three days. Along the way, we would usually drive through Yellowstone National Park, which meant we only had a couple more hours of driving before arriving in my dad's hometown of four hundred people.

A few of those memories include riding around with my grandpa on his red Farmall tractor, sitting at the breakfast table eating Grandma's homemade bread and strawberry jam, and making paper boats to float down the irrigation canal across the street.

But perhaps one of my best memories is finding a pile of old, rusted-out Tonka trucks under some lilac bushes in their backyard. These toys belonged to my Uncle Vernon, the youngest of my dad's siblings. When I stumbled across them at perhaps five or six years old, it was like finding a long-lost treasure. I would spend hours filling up the dump truck with dirt, unloading the dirt, and then smoothing out the transported dirt with the big grader.

Years later, Uncle Vernon recalled his own fond memories of playing in the dirt with those trucks and my dad getting down on his hands and knees to play with him. You see, when Vernon was only five years old, my dad, Ken, was eighteen and getting ready to head off to college; it was 1969.

To this day, my dad and uncle maintain a close relationship that goes back to those special bonding times in the dirt. Dad wasn't afraid to get dirty in order to make those memories with his little brother. Though thirteen years separated them, those Tonka trucks put them on equal ground.

Isn't this what Jesus did when he stepped into our world?

As John 1:14 tells us, "So the Word became human and made his home among us. He was full of unfailing love and faithfulness. And we have seen his glory, the glory of the Father's one and only Son."

The Message translation puts it this way:
The Word became flesh and blood,
and moved into the neighborhood.
We saw the glory with our own eyes,
the one-of-a-kind glory,
like Father, like Son,
Generous inside and out,
true from start to finish.

"Moved into the neighborhood." I like that! Jesus decided to get down on his hands and knees in order to play Tonka trucks with us. He wanted to bond with us and show us a glimpse of his Father. He wasn't afraid to get dirty in the process even though he was without sin. "For we do not have a high priest who is unable to empathize with our weaknesses, but we have one who has been tempted in every way, just as we are—yet he did not sin" (Hebrews 4:15 NIV).

For thirty-three years, Jesus showed us what living life to the fullest looks like. He touched lepers, ate with sinners, gave sight to the blind, and stood up to religious bullies even though it led to him being crucified on a Roman cross. His death and resurrection provided the means by which we will one day step into his neighborhood for eternity.

I imagine Jesus has a pretty cool Tonka truck collection in heaven.

Reflection: Think of the person who's reflected the face of Jesus in your life. How can you thank them today?

DAY 5
"C" Students vs.
"A" Students

Read: Matthew 4:18–22

Up until the second quarter of my eighth grade year, I garnered my fair share of Cs in school. My grade point average went from 2.7 the first quarter to 3.63 the second quarter. Why the sudden improvement? My mom motivated me more than she ever could have imagined by telling me that college basketball scouts looked at the grades of players all the way back to the middle school years.

This wasn't completely accurate information, but it worked. Though I still had a C from time to time, they came fewer and further between. Back in those days, I ate, drank, and slept basketball, and my dream was to play in college and eventually the NBA (didn't happen). My grades weren't going to stand in the way of that dream.

It was similar for teens back when Jesus was alive. Jewish boys and girls would often attend school until age ten where they would literally memorize the Torah, the first five books of the Old Testament. From this point, only the best and brightest boys would go to the next level where they would study the rest of the Old Testament Scriptures until age thirteen or fourteen.

And finally, only the cream of the crop would be chosen to "follow" the local rabbi. This elite group of disciples would go where he went and eat what he ate—modeling their lives after the rabbi. Those who didn't make the previous cuts would pick up the trades of their fathers, whether it was carpentry, sheepherding, or fishing.

Guys like Simon, Andrew, James, and John hadn't made the cut. So instead of following the local rabbi, they were down by the docks, working the family business. It's interesting that Jesus went after men the local rabbi had rejected. Instead of targeting the cream-of-the-crop, straight-A students, Jesus offered his invitation, "Follow Me," to former C students. They would become followers of the ultimate Rabbi.

Can you imagine schools like Harvard or Yale going after C students? Once again, this sort of math wouldn't fly in today's competitive, dog-eat-dog society.

No wonder Matthew 4:20 says these guys left their nets at once and followed him. They were being given an opportunity they thought was lost. To follow a rabbi in Jewish society was the greatest of honors.

The qualifications for Jesus's honor society are different from the world's, and I couldn't be more grateful!

Reflection: Has there ever been a time in your life when you didn't make the cut? Think of some specific instances where you failed to measure up to a certain standard. Now bring those to Jesus one by one.

A few of those memories include riding around with my grandpa on his red Farmall tractor, sitting at the breakfast table eating Grandma's homemade bread

DAY 6
All-You-Can-Eat
Fish Sandwiches

Read: John 6:1–14

Jesus and his disciples found themselves out in the boonies where restaurants were sparse. No McDonald's in sight. This wouldn't have been a big deal if it was merely Jesus and his twelve closest friends, but there was also a "huge crowd" among them. There may well have been over fifteen thousand men, women, and children out there since five thousand men alone were officially counted (v. 10).

Where's a food court or a Walmart when you need one? Jesus asked Philip something along those lines: "Where can we buy bread to feed all these people?" (v. 5).

The shocked disciples did a quick food inventory before Andrew stepped forward with his report: "There's a young boy here with five barley loaves and two fish. But what good is that with this huge crowd?" (v. 9).

Seems pretty insignificant, huh? A young boy holding a meager supply among a hungry horde of thousands. Except on this day, the Bread of Life was among them.

What Jesus proceeded to do next was teach these young grasshoppers another divine math lesson. Class was in session.

The food critic reviews started steadily streaming in.

"Compliments to the Chef!"

"Best fish sandwich of AD 31!"

"A refreshing lesson in multiplication!"

"The best in divine dining."

"No better deal for the money."

When all the dust settled and belly groans were exchanged for belches of contentment, "They all ate as much as they wanted. After everyone was full, Jesus told his disciples, 'Now gather the leftovers, so that nothing is wasted.' So they picked up the pieces and filled twelve baskets with scraps left by the people who had eaten from the five barley loaves" (v. 11–13).

We're not exactly sure how the disciples managed to obtain the young boy's bounty. Did they make a deal with him? Sack-lunch bully tactics? I personally believe he willingly offered the Rabbi what he had in his hands without charge. From there, Jesus multiplied his generous offering.

Like the boy, if you and I are willing to offer our lives to the Rabbi, multiplication can take place. On our own, we may feel insignificant. When Jesus is added to the equation, our lives become like an all-you-can-eat buffet that satisfies all those we encounter. And with Jesus, nothing in our lives is wasted (v. 12).

Bon appétit!

Reflection: Can you think of a time when you witnessed Jesus multiplying something before your eyes? What are the "loaves and fishes" you can offer freely to the Rabbi today?

DAY 7
Two Regrets,
Two Responses

Read: Matthew 26:69–27:10

There are few things that drain the life out of a person like regret. I once heard someone say, "If you ever find yourself in the city of regret, make it a brief visit rather than a permanent residence."

We've all done things (or not done things) that we regret, and many of us have beaten ourselves black-and-blue by rehashing these regrets in our minds as if they're an endless play loop.

In 2 Corinthians 7:10 (NIV), Paul writes, "Godly sorrow brings repentance that leads to salvation and leaves no regret, but worldly sorrow brings death."

Regret implies an uneasiness about something in the past that we're not proud of. But repentance is turning from that thing we're not proud of and turning to a forgiving Father.

Peter and Judas walked closely with Jesus for three years. They heard incredible teachings, witnessed miraculous healings, and saw demons fleeing.

In the end, all these wonderful things weren't enough to prevent Peter and Judas from denying and betraying their Master. Peter, the burly fisherman who boldly vowed never to deny Jesus, even unto death, was reduced to cowardice by servant girls who confronted him. Judas, never one to pass on making (or stealing) a buck, was happy to betray the Son of God for a mere thirty pieces of silver (roughly $400 based on the value of silver today).

And they both hated themselves for it.

While it's easy to point a finger at these men, we all have some of Peter and Judas inside us. Ultimately, we can learn a valuable lesson as we look more closely at the way each of them dealt with his regret.

We see proof of Peter's regret when we read that he "wept bitterly" after denying he knew Jesus for a third time (Matthew 26:75 NIV). No doubt he was feeling pretty down on himself, as we all would be. That could have been the end of Peter's story if not for that wonderful exchange with the resurrected Jesus on the shores of Galilee (John 21).

Peter made the decision to repent after being forgiven and restored by Jesus. We simply need to read Acts, 1 Peter, and 2 Peter to see the fruit of his repentance.

Judas similarly regretted his own act of betraying Jesus. We read that he was "filled with remorse" (Matthew 27:3) after realizing his Rabbi had been condemned to die. We can even point to some evidence of repentance as he decided to return the silver he was paid. Unfortunately, rather than continue down the road of repentance, Judas chose to end his life (Matthew 27:5).

When you and I choose to stay in the uneasiness of regret, we are choosing the way of Judas and harming ourselves. By choosing the way of Peter, we're able to be fully restored and given a fresh start.

In some ways, I feel sorry for the way things ended for Judas. We see Jesus extending grace to him right up to the kiss of betrayal when he said, "My friend, go ahead and do what you have come for" (Matthew 26:50).

My friend.

Yes, it was already prophesied that Judas would betray his Lord. But isn't it like the Son of God to extend his friendship during our darkest, most sinful hours?

Let's make repentance and restoration our destination.

Reflection: This quote by Fulton Oursler really hits home, "Many of us crucify ourselves between two thieves—regret for the past and fear of the future." Can you relate to either of these? How do the responses of Peter and Judas impact your own response?

DAY 8
Calm, Cool, and Collected

Read: Mark 4:35–41

What or who comes to mind when you think of the phrase "calm, cool, and collected"? Perhaps Tom Brady leading his team in the final minutes of the Super Bowl. Simone Biles nailing a gymnastics routine on her way to an Olympic gold medal. Kobe Bryant charging with the basketball as the clock winds down.

Some may even think of various actors or actresses like James Dean, Steve McQueen (known as the King of Cool), Paul Newman (Cool Hand Luke) Angelina Jolie, Brad Pitt, Clint Eastwood, or Emma Watson, to name just a few.

We might refer to someone as being "cool as a cucumber" for their calm demeanor under pressure. For those old enough to remember, there was a 1960s commercial for Secret brand deodorant that promised to control perspiration while keeping the user "cool, calm, and collected."

In today's passage from Scripture, we see the essence of calm, cool, and collected as Jesus sleeps (with his head on a cushion perhaps) at the back of a boat as a "fierce storm" rages on the Sea of Galilee (v. 37). Many of those in the boat were experienced fishermen who had seen a storm or two in their lifetimes, but this one was a doozy. These grown men were scared and for good reason.

This body of water is the lowest freshwater lake on earth at about 700 feet below sea level. Sudden storms are known to stir up waves quickly on this bowl full of water that measures 33 miles wide, 13 miles long, and 140 feet deep.

For Jesus, it's hakuna matata (Swahili for "no worries" or "no troubles") as he snores away.

When the frantic ex-fishermen finally wake Jesus from his sweet dream, the Son of God commands "Silence [or Peace]! Be still!" (v. 39). The Greek word used here is phimoo, which comes from the word phimos and means "to close the mouth with a muzzle." Like an owner muzzling their aggressive dog, Jesus muzzles this unruly storm. Aren't we all a bit agitated after being suddenly woken from deep sleep?

In a split second, the weather went from gusty to glassy on Galilee. And in a split second, the disciples realized more than ever that Jesus was more than just a Teacher from Nazareth.

When the Son of God is in our boat, we have access to the One who is able to bring peace to any circumstance. In Christ, the forecast is always calm, cool, and collected.

Reflection: What kinds of "fierce storms" have you seen Jesus calm in your own life? Spend some time thanking him for all the times he's saved you from drowning and being overtaken by the waves of life.

DAY 9
From Outcast to Evangelist

Read: Mark 5:1–20

I was perhaps eleven or twelve years old when my dad came home one evening with some somber news. "They found Claude under a bridge this morning . . . he was frozen as hard as an ice cube."

Those words continue to ring in my ears all these years later. Claude was a homeless man who wandered in and out of our small southern Oregon logging town while riding an old ten-speed bicycle and carrying the biggest pack of earthly possessions you can imagine. I'm still amazed the man could pedal his bike without falling over under that load.

I'm sad to say that my friends and I referred to him as Dirt Claude due to the fact that he was filthy and carried the stench of someone who rarely saw a shower or bath. Though he couldn't have been more than thirty years old, Claude was missing nearly all of his teeth. This didn't prevent him from indulging in large wads of chewing tobacco, witnessed by the dark brown juices that dripped off his chin.

My dad chose to still show Claude dignity as a human being. If he saw Claude pedaling through town, he would pull his pickup to the side of the road where the two would talk for fifteen or twenty minutes. Before parting ways, Dad would almost always slip a twenty-dollar bill into Claude's hand. I know because I would usually watch while slinking down into my seat for fear of being seen by my friends.

My compassionate dad might have been the last kind face Claude saw before succumbing to the elements on a cold and lonely winter night. My father's actions eventually planted seeds of tenderness in my own heart toward those considered outcasts in society.

Remember that "fierce storm" Jesus calmed in yesterday's reading? Upon landing on the other side of the lake, Jesus and his disciples encountered a screaming maniac who wasn't exactly helping the local tourism industry. No one had any answers for this man consumed by his own internal storm. It was a full-blown category 5 hurricane.

When Jesus asked the man his name, an eerie voice answered, "Legion," which indicated the amount of demons who took up residence inside. A typical Roman legion was made up of five thousand soldiers. Could it be that there were that many unclean spirits inside this poor guy? Regardless of the number, what kind of power had to be behind a man who could snap chains and smash shackles intended to subdue him?

At this point, I would have been hightailing it back to the boat. But the Son of God was about to calm his second storm of the day. In an instant, the demonic horde was evicted from their human house and now found themselves flying with pigs into the water. You might even call it the Great Swine Dive.

How do you repay someone who has taken you from a life of insanity to instant sanity? From being possessed to now being blessed? From hopeless to healed? With tears in your eyes, you beg and plead with the Teacher to allow you to follow him to the ends of the earth.

"No," Jesus said. "I've had special plans for you all along. You're going to stay quite busy sharing your story with everyone here in this region."

Only with Jesus is it possible to go from outcast to evangelist in mere minutes.

Reflection: Do you know anyone like Claude in your area? How can you bring Jesus to the shores of outcasts in your neck of the woods?

DAY 10
Here Today,
Gone Tomorrow

Read: John 11:1–44

Life isn't fair. In fact, sometimes it can seem downright cruel with its myriad of unexpected twists and turns. On average, over 150,000 people die each day. That's nearly two people every second. Death in and of itself isn't unexpected. We all have an appointment with the dreaded "D word" whether we want it or not (Hebrews 9:27). As comedian Woody Allen once said, "It's not that I'm afraid to die, I just don't want to be there when it happens."

Even as I write these words, the world is grieving the unexpected death of former basketball star Kobe Bryant who perished in a helicopter accident along with eight others (including his daughter). How could someone so full of life suddenly be gone? At forty-one years young, this living legend was just getting started on the next season of life. One day he's congratulating LeBron James who passed him for third place on the all-time NBA scoring list. The next day he's gone.

Death doesn't play favorites. It's no respecter of persons. It doesn't care whether you're wealthy or poor. It comes knocking on every door, including yours and mine. It came knocking on my grandpa's door less than a year ago. There's a good chance that you've also lost someone in the past year that you loved deeply.

In today's story from Scripture, it seems that Lazarus was a man who was loved by many. The more we love someone, the more difficult it is to lose them. Lazarus's sisters, Mary and Martha, were shaken to the core. But they weren't the only ones weeping that day. In the shortest verse recorded in the Bible, we read these two words: "Jesus wept" (John 11:35 NIV).

Yes, the Son of God was a blubbering mess of tears. It was very evident to those nearby how much Jesus loved his friend Laz. I'm so grateful that God doesn't hide these displays of emotion. From cover to cover, the Bible is real and raw.

Thankfully, death doesn't have the final word for those in Christ. Jesus utters the following hope-filled words not only to Martha but also to you and me: "I am the resurrection and the life. Anyone who believes in me will live, even after dying. Everyone who lives in me and believes in me will never ever die" (John 11:25–26).

I've always wondered how ole Laz felt about returning from the dead only to endure more pain in life and eventually see death come knocking a second time. Regardless, it was a small price to pay in return for the lives that were impacted and the glory it brought Jesus.

For those who call upon Jesus as their only hope beyond the grave, these words of Billy Graham sum it up well: "Someday you will read or hear that Billy Graham is dead. Don't you believe a word of it. I shall be more alive than I am now. I will just have changed my address. I will have gone into the presence of God."

Reflection: Ecclesiastes 7:4 says, "A wise person thinks a lot about death, while a fool thinks only about having a good time." Why is it wise to think about our own appointment with death?

DAY 11
Taking the Fall

Read: Luke 23:32–43

Everyone loves a winner whether we're talking about sports teams racking up championships or companies earning huge profits. But when losses start piling up, fingers begin pointing. In the case of sports teams, those fingers usually point toward the head coach. With companies, it's the president or CEO under the microscope.

Many of us have used this same logic to shake our fists toward God. We see the "losses" piling up all around the world, and we wonder what the CEO of the universe plans to do about it. If we don't see the results we're looking for, we decide to fire him, at least in our minds anyway.

In today's passage, we see the King of Kings being mocked by three different groups of people. It began with the religious elite as they scoffed at this Teacher who was wrecking their comfortable business. Then we see the Roman soldiers getting in on the mocking, thrilled to put away another Jewish troublemaker.

Finally, one of the condemned criminals decided to use his final hours to scoff at the so-called Messiah.

All three groups challenged Jesus to save himself if he truly was who he said he was. Little did they know this was all part of the Plan of all plans. Jesus had already forgiven their ignorance (Luke 23:34). Rather than save himself, Jesus would buy the salvation for mankind that only his blood could pay for.

God takes sin very seriously. All we need to do is read Leviticus 16 to get a glimpse of that seriousness. In Jewish tradition, each year on the Day of Atonement (Yom Kippur), a "scapegoat" was released into the wilderness after the high priest symbolically laid the sins of the people upon the goat, thus carrying these "sins upon itself into a desolate land" (Leviticus 16:22).

Imagine the Son of God becoming our scapegoat and taking our sins into a "desolate land" never to be seen again. Imagine this eternal High Priest (Hebrews 4:14–15) willingly becoming our sacrifice in order to cleanse us of all our lies, lust, and lawlessness.

Getting back to our fist-shaking and finger-pointing, what's God's plan for all these losses that are stacking up? A better question might be, What has he already done?

Paul said it well in his second letter to the Corinthians: "For God made Christ, who never sinned, to be the offering for our sin, so that we could be made right with God through Christ" (2 Corinthians 5:21).

All he did was pay off our debt, right our wrongs, take our bullet, and serve our death sentence.

He took the fall.

Reflection: Have you ever found yourself shaking your fists at God? Spend some time thanking Jesus for being your sin offering. "Father, forgive me, for I don't always know what I'm doing."

DAY 12
How Bad Do You Want It?

by Gwen Ebner

Read: Mark 7:31–37

Have you ever been asked, "How bad do you want it?" At times, it may be important to answer this question because there may be a cost to the thing you want. It could be money, hard work, embarrassment, or even the need to surrender having it your way.

In Mark 7, we find a story about a man who has a surprise encounter with Jesus. He's brought to Jesus because he is deaf and can hardly speak. The people beg Jesus to heal him (v. 32).

How would it feel to be deaf and dumb and have someone take you to Jesus?

How does Jesus heal the man?

The first thing Jesus does is lead the man away from the crowd. Often Jesus invites us to leave the noise and craziness of life in order to be with him as he does his work in us. Next we observe Jesus healing the man in an unusual way, by spitting on his fingers and touching the man's tongue (v. 33).

Has healing ever come to you in a different way than you expected?

Why did Jesus do such an odd thing?

- Maybe Jesus needed to see how bad this man wanted to be healed.

- Or possibly Jesus could have wanted time alone with the man,

- Also, if we look at the customs of Jewish culture, we find that they believed the saliva of a firstborn son had the power to heal. Jesus may have been trying to connect with something the deaf man already understood.

Would you allow Jesus to do something strange like this in order to heal you?

Then Jesus looked up to heaven signifying that his power came from God. And as he did this, he also deeply sighed. Possibly Jesus's sigh was expressing his grief over the suffering the man had experienced. It could also have been a prayer, within itself, just like when the Spirit intercedes for us with sighs or groans that cannot be expressed in words (Romans 8:26).

Finally, Jesus speaks one word, "Ephphatha," an Aramaic word meaning "Be opened" (v. 34). Immediately the man's tongue is freed, and he begins to speak plainly (v. 35).

In this story I sense Jesus asking us two questions: "How bad do you want to grow or be healed? And would you be willing to allow me, Jesus, to do something odd or embarrassing in order to heal or transform your life?" I guess it all depends on this question: how bad do we really want it?

Reflection: When was the last time you wanted something so badly you were willing to allow Jesus to take you through any process necessary to receive it?

This devotion was a guest contribution by Dr. Gwen Ebner, who just happens to be my mother-in-law. To find out more about Gwen's ministry, including her books and speaking, visit www.GwenEbner.com

DAY 13
Faithfulness > Feelings

Read: Luke 9:51; 22:39–46

If I'm honest, I would say I've been jerked around by my feelings for much of my life. I feel like eating a large piece of carrot cake. I don't feel like doing a hard workout today. This weather makes me feel depressed. I don't feel like going to church this week. I'll see how I feel tomorrow. Know the feeling?

Feelings can lead to hasty decisions that we soon regret. We do whatever feels good in the moment and gives us that short-term gratification. Feelings, like the weather here in Colorado, can go from one extreme to another in the span of five minutes.

Faithfulness, on the other hand, is in it for the long haul. It's like an anchor that keeps a ship steady regardless of the surroundings. Faithfulness doesn't have a Plan B in its back pocket in case things don't work out. Instead, faithfulness is the plan whether we feel like it or not.

In Luke 9:51 we read, "As the time drew near for him to ascend to heaven, Jesus resolutely set out for Jerusalem" (emphasis mine).

Some translations use the phrase "set his face" instead of the word resolutely. It comes from the Greek sterizo, which means "to set fast; confirm; fix, establish, steadfast, set, strengthen."

In other words, Jesus was dead set on making his way toward the "the city that kills the prophets and stones God's messengers" (Luke 13:34).

Still, Jesus had real feelings just like you and I. Though he was God in the flesh, he was also fully human. He faced the full range of emotions and temptations that we encounter daily (Hebrews 4:15).

We see the feelings of the Son of God on full display in the Garden of Gethsemane: "'Father, if you are willing, please take this cup of suffering away from me. Yet I want your will to be done, not mine.' Then an angel from heaven appeared and strengthened him. He prayed more fervently, and he was in such agony of spirit that his sweat fell to the ground like great drops of blood" (Luke 22:42–44).

Cup of suffering. Agony of spirit. Sweat like great drops of blood. Doesn't sound very appealing, does it? We won't find these descriptions in a Caribbean cruise brochure.

Yet Jesus demonstrates that prayer is a powerful weapon to help us overcome our own feelings. After he prayed, "an angel from heaven appeared and strengthened him" (Luke 22:43). As you and I pray, we're also given strength to endure our fickle feelings.

Ever since Adam and Eve were banished from the garden of Eden, humans have been trying to get back to paradise on earth by any means possible. But the only way back to Eden is through Gethsemane. The only way back to our Father is through the Son.

I'm so grateful Jesus chose faithfulness over feelings.

Reflection: Have you been tossed and turned by your own feelings? Join me in this prayer, "Father, please grant me the strength to overcome feelings that betray me. I want to be resolute in remaining faithful to the plans you have for me. In Jesus's name, amen."

DAY 14
Weight Lifted

Read: Matthew 18:21–35

Upon graduating from college in May of 1996, I was staring at some debt I had accrued in addition to my school loans. This additional debt of $13,000 consisted of two credit cards I had maxed out, a used car loan, and a loan from one of my best friends. The credit card debt was basically $7,500 of unwise, wasteful spending. I'm embarrassed to say that I would then take out cash advances in order to make the minimum monthly payment. I was one of those suckers whom credit card companies salivate over.

After returning home that following summer, my dad asked me a question that caught me off guard: "Aunt Vera wants to know if you need anything." I had a hunch this question might mean more than a few pairs of socks since she had recently blessed Dad with a brand-new 1996 Toyota Tacoma pickup. So I half-jokingly responded, "I sure could use about $13,000 to pay off some debt."

The next day, my seventy-nine-year-old aunt told me to stop by her house, which was only a few blocks away. After coming inside and sitting down at her kitchen table, she asked, "Sweetie, your dad mentioned some debt you'd like to pay off. How much was that again?" "Um, thirteen thousand," I sheepishly responded.

And then she proceeded to write out a check for thirteen thousand bones before sliding it across the table to me. All I could do was sit there stunned. Eventually I went over to give her a big hug. In an instant a weight was lifted.

Just a few months later, my feisty Aunt Vera was gone. It seems that her instincts told her she wasn't going to be here much longer, which put her in a giving mood. To this day, her lavish gift remains one of the most vivid pictures that I have of grace and forgiveness. Simply put, I received something good that I didn't deserve.

In today's encounter with the Teacher, Jesus is giving Peter a lesson on forgiveness. He compares the kingdom of heaven to a man who was indebted up to his eyeballs to his king, owing him "millions of dollars," or ten thousand talents as it says in the Greek (v. 24).

It turns out that one talent was worth about twenty years of wages for a laborer. So ten thousand talents equaled two hundred thousand years of wages! Put another way, ten thousand talents equated to about 375 tons of silver. In case you forgot, one ton equals two thousand pounds. As of this writing, an ounce of silver is selling for $17.55. There are sixteen ounces in a pound. After crunching some numbers, we come up with $210,600,000 in today's value.

And would you believe that this king completely forgave the man's debt? Unfortunately, this guy had a case of forgiveness amnesia when it came time to collect "a few thousand dollars" that a fellow servant owed him (v. 28).

I'm afraid you and I have experienced that same amnesia in our own lives, if we're honest. Someone wrongs us and we want to grab them by the throat, all too quickly forgetting how much we've wronged a perfect and holy God.

Earthly debts pale in comparison to heavenly debts. It took a divine Being to pay a divine debt in full.

That's the ultimate weight lifted.

Reflection: Describe the feeling of being on the receiving end of lavish grace or forgiveness. Whose burden could you help lift today by sharing these three powerful words: "I forgive you"?

DAY 15
Wounded Warriors

Read: John 20:24–29

I remember it like it was yesterday even though it happened forty years ago. The bell rang signaling the end of recess for our first grade class. In the hustle and bustle of lining up in front of our classroom door, I felt a sharp pain in the palm of my left hand. I had accidentally been stabbed with a freshly sharpened pencil by a student who apparently forgot one of the cardinal rules of recess: No pencils allowed on the playground!

When I look down at my left palm all these years later, I can still see a faint black dot from where the lead tip broke off. Thankfully, I haven't yet keeled over from lead poisoning.

Whether we're kids or adults, there's something satisfying about showing others our "battle scars" and recounting the stories attached to them. Old football injuries, bicycle wrecks, falls from bunk beds, road rash, tumbles on the trail, dog bites, and cat scratches. Each of our bodies bares the proof of our mishaps.

Young Thomas wanted some proof. It seems that this doubting disciple missed out on one of the first post-resurrection appearances by Jesus that Peter, John, and the others were raving about. I'm sure they tried every which way to convince Thomas, but he wasn't having any of it. "I won't believe it unless I see the nail wounds in his hands, put my fingers into them, and place my hand into the wound in his side" (v. 25).

Could it be that we walk past people every day who refuse to believe unless they see our wounds? We all carry spiritual and emotional scars along with the physical ones mentioned above. When we're real and authentic about our past and present struggles, we help create a bridge to the hearts of people who, like Thomas, struggle with doubt.

Eight days later, Thomas would have his own encounter with the risen Rabbi. The Son of God was more than willing to allow Thomas to touch the wounds that ultimately bought his freedom. There's something powerful when we can say we've personally encountered Jesus.

Perhaps when others see that we've been wounded and yet stand unashamed to reveal those healed wounds, they too might eventually exclaim, like Thomas, "My Lord and my God!" (v. 28, emphasis mine).

Some of us have taken the best shot the devil could give us and yet we still stand by the power of Jesus. This speaks volumes to those watching and waiting from a distance.

We're wounded warriors on display for all to see.

Reflection: Think of the people you most often cross paths with (neighbors, coworkers, family members, church acquaintances, etc.). Would they say that you're real and authentic? Why is it so difficult for us to display our wounds in person or on social media?

DAY 16
Mending Messiah

Read: Luke 6:6–11; 13:10–17

Over the years, I've developed an attachment to various articles of clothing that I can't bring myself to throw away despite the wear and tear. A pair of Eddie Bauer flannel-lined pants with holes worn on the backside. A pair of black Nike sweatpants that needed a new drawstring due to a decreased waist size (good problem). A Brooks long-sleeve running top with a tear in the left cuff.

These are just a few items that my seamstress friend Lisha has been able to mend and restore since I stumbled upon her services several years ago. Her sewing skills have breathed new life into worn-out clothing that had seen better days.

In today's readings, Luke, the physician, shares two encounters involving the Great Physician. Both stories share several things in common:

- Both included broken, damaged human beings in need of mending.

- Both encounters occurred on the Sabbath.

- Both occurred in local synagogues.

- Jesus healed both individuals even though neither asked for it.

- Both healings enraged the religious elite.

It's safe to say both healing recipients were glad they came to church that day.

Based on the similarities above, we see that the Son of God relishes the opportunity to bless people seven days a week, which includes the Sabbath. In fact, just prior to restoring the man's deformed right hand, Jesus proclaimed himself to be "Lord, even over the Sabbath" (Luke 6:5).

Imagine being bent over double for eighteen years without the ability to stand up straight. The word that Dr. Luke uses to describe this poor woman's condition is astheneia, which means "lack of strength, weakness, infirmity." Just as painful would have been the disapproving looks and whispers by onlookers. Eighteen days, let alone years, would have seemed like a lifetime.

These two encounters remind us that brokenness is difficult to escape in this life. Physical illnesses like the flu, injuries, infections, diseases, and the effects of aging eventually hit everyone. Brokenness shows up in other ways like addiction and depression. There's brokenness in relationships in the form of dishonesty, unfaithfulness, gossip, betrayal, abuse, loss, and divorce.

Jesus is still in the business of breathing new life into worn-out people who have seen better days. He's still delivering people from addiction and abuse. He's still knitting people back together physically, mentally, emotionally, and spiritually.

He's the mending Messiah.

Reflection: How have you seen Jesus mend your own life? Just as Jesus noticed the brokenness of the crippled man and woman, ask him to give you eyes to notice those near you who are broken and in need of mending.

DAY 17
Out on a Limb

Read: Luke 19:1–10

If you attended Sunday school as a child, you might recall singing a cute little song about a guy named Zacchaeus. Here's the first verse to jog your memory:

> Zacchaeus was a wee little man,
>
> And a wee little man was he.
>
> He climbed up in a sycamore tree
>
> For the Lord he wanted to see.

As a kid, I loved this song because I also loved climbing trees. There were several options right out our back door that I took full advantage of. My favorite was a tall fir tree that I would climb over fifty feet up in order to reach a particular sturdy limb. There, I would position myself on the limb with my back against the tree trunk, pull out my PB&J sandwich, and enjoy the unique view from my lofty position.

Our "wee little man'" above must have been desperate for a better view of this Rabbi rolling through town. It wasn't often that chief tax collectors were known to climb trees. Though short in stature, Zacchaeus wasn't short on cash as a tax man working for the Romans. His name would have been a curse word to those living in Jericho. If I'm honest, I've probably viewed the letters IRS in a similar fashion.

Imagine the shock this wee little scoundrel must have felt when the Master looked up and called him . . . wait for it . . . by name! He would have been familiar with people calling him all sorts of things other than his name. Deep down, Zacchaeus knew he wasn't living up to his name, which means "pure, innocent."

One encounter with Jesus would change all of that. Unlike the rich man Jesus had encountered just prior (Luke 18:18–30), Zacchaeus wouldn't walk away sad. Instead, he would come alive for the first time. Giving away half his wealth, and repaying those he cheated four times the amount he'd taken from them, was the least he could do.

Even more than living up to his name, Zacchaeus was finally living up to his heritage as a "true son [descendant] of Abraham" (Luke 19:9). Just like father Abraham was called out by Yahweh to move in a new direction, the tax man was being called by Yeshua (Messiah) to a change of heart that would lead to a new way of doing business.

There's always a risk of falling and getting hurt when you're out on a limb . . . unless Jesus is waiting with open arms at the bottom.

Reflection: Think back to the first time you were desperate to get a closer look at Jesus. How has your life changed since then?

DAY 18
What a Waste!

Read: Matthew 26:6–13; Mark 14:3–9; Luke 7:36–50; John 12:1–8

Have you ever watched someone squander something worth a lot of money? That's what seemed to be happening on this evening when Jesus was hanging with some locals over dinner. Almost out of nowhere, this woman came up to Jesus and began pouring nearly a pint of really expensive perfume over Jesus's head and feet.

In case you forgot, a pint equals sixteen ounces. Have you bought perfume or cologne lately? You practically have to open a Swiss bank account just to smell good! After you've made this costly purchase (usually over fifty dollars these days), you're left standing there with a little glass bottle holding no more than one to two ounces, if you're lucky. How many lawns would a person have to mow to make that amount of cash?

Picture this woman dumping several of those little glass bottles all over Jesus's head and feet. Even those closest to Jesus denounced this as an act of irresponsibility. A squandering of over a year's wages, according to others. Some even argued the perfume could have been sold in order to help the poor (ah, the classic guilt trip).

And Jesus? What's his take? He praises her! He has nothing but praise for this woman's reckless extravagance. Pure and utter wastefulness, and Jesus eats it up! Another example of the upside-down math of Jesus.

Whether it's time, perfume, or money, you and I could never waste enough of it on the Son of God. There's no greater return on investment (ROI) than blowing our hard-earned income on the kingdom of God.

What looked like a year's worth of wages going up in smoke was a sweet aroma of sacrifice wafting into the nostrils of God. Like an eternal air freshener was this woman's gift to the Giver of life. The fact that all four Gospels refer to this act should compel us to consider its impact.

Only heaven knows the full impact as you and I pour out our lives to Jesus as an act of "wasteful" worship.

Reflection: Mother Teresa once said, "A sacrifice to be real must cost, must hurt, and must empty ourselves." Have you exhibited this level of sacrifice in your own life or witnessed it in the lives of others?

DAY 19
Healing Touch

Read: Mark 5:25–34

When I was in high school, basketball was everything to me. I was even known to sleep with my basketball. Imagine my dismay when I developed a lower back issue my sophomore year that had the ability to stop me, literally, in my tracks. It was a sharp, jarring sensation at the point where the back meets the hip area. It didn't occur every day, but it was always at the back of my mind. It was usually a quick movement or explosive jump that would trigger it.

It finally came to a head during my junior year when I needed to sit out two games due to a painful flare-up. My parents decided to take me to a local chiropractor named Dr. Parsons who was seventy-two years old and blind. Though I was a bit skeptical, I was also desperate to find a solution.

As I lay on his examination table, he slowly felt up and down my spine, hips, knees, and feet. After a few minutes, he said, "You need orthotics." He proceeded to take molds of my feet before sending them off to have customized orthotics made.

A week later the orthotics arrived at his office, and I went down to try them out. Almost instantly I could feel a difference. Over the course of the next week, my lower back issue was resolved as the orthotics did their magical work of realigning things. I was so over-joyed that I could have kissed Dr. Parsons over and over again.

In today's story from Scripture, we see a woman who had gone to every doctor and specialist under the sun in order to find a solution to the "constant bleeding" she'd endured for over twelve years (v. 25). In her frantic search, she was left with no answers, an empty bank account, and very little hope.

Her bleeding condition put this poor woman in quite a predicament. According to Leviticus 15:25, "If a woman has a flow of blood for many days that is un-related to her menstrual period, or if the blood con-tinues beyond the normal period, she is ceremonially unclean. As during her menstrual period, the woman will be unclean as long as the discharge continues."

Anything she touched would be considered unclean. If anyone else touched something she touched, they would also be unclean until they took a bath and changed clothes. Being "unclean" meant you weren't allowed anywhere near a synagogue or temple. It was basically a twelve-year quarantine for this woman.

It's easy to understand how desperate she was when she took the risk of a lifetime by pushing her way through a crowd surrounding a Teacher named Jesus. Contaminating these people for a day would be a small price to pay in order to reach this Healer she had heard so much about. With every last bit of faith and hope she had left, she reached out to touch the Rabbi's robe.

In an instant, Jesus put a stop to twelve years of physical, emotional, and spiritual misery. Though completely healed, she wasn't going to be "stealing" any miracles from the Son of God that day. Jesus looked this woman lovingly in the eye and publicly proclaimed her to be clean. No more hiding. No more expensive trips to the doctor.

One encounter with the Great Physician can change everything.

Reflection: What is it in your life that you've exhausted all your resources trying to fix? It could be physical, mental, emotional, or spiritual in nature. In quiet desperation, push your way 'through the crowd' in order to bring your issue to Jesus.

DAY 20
Sinking Feeling

Read: Matthew 14:22–33

As I write this, the coronavirus, also known as COVID-19, has gripped our nation and world. The fear and panic are palpable, like cutting through a stick of butter. The last time I recall us being on edge like this was after 9/11. This feels different, however, as people frantically hoard things like toilet paper and peanut butter in preparation for the great hunkering in.

In today's story from Scripture, we read about the disciples being in trouble as heavy winds were stirring up waves on the lake. As they were fighting to stay afloat, Jesus comes walking toward them on the water. Now they were really freaked out, thinking they're seeing a ghost!

Jesus reassures them with these tender words: "Don't be afraid. . . . Take courage. I am here!" (v. 27). Peter, ready to take a walk on water himself, jumps overboard (with Jesus's encouragement) and slowly makes his way toward the Master. Things are going well until . . . the "Rock" starts sinking.

Peter began taking on panic and doubt faster than the boat was taking on water. The strong wind and waves were overwhelming. Terrifying. Jesus was now an afterthought as mere survival became the priority. With one last gasp, the feisty fisherman cries out, "Save me, Lord!" (v. 30). Like the eternal lifeguard that he is, Jesus reaches out to grab a panicking Peter.

And this same Jesus is ready to meet you and me right in the middle of any storm we might face. Whether it's a literal storm like a tornado in Tennessee or an infectious storm like the coronavirus, we can grab the hand of the Prince of Peace. I can't guarantee that any of us will wake up tomorrow, but after nearly thirty years of walking with Jesus, I know there is One who holds our future.

As we utter our own desperate "Save me, Lord!" cries, he'll meet us in the midst of the wind and waves.

There's no need to let panic pull us under when the Son of God offers us a life jacket of peace.

Reflection: When the coronavirus began dominating news and social media, how did you respond? On a scale of one to ten, where was your panic level? "Jesus, we reach out and take your strong hand of rescue. We trust that you're in full control of every circumstance we face. In Jesus's name, amen."

DAY 21
Don't Lose Heart

Read: Luke 18:1–8

In the movie Braveheart, there's a powerful moment where Robert the Bruce is talking with his leprous father with tears clouding his eyes. After betraying William Wallace (Mel Gibson's character) on the battlefield at Falkirk, Robert is now laden with guilt.

He tells his father, "Men follow me, because if they don't, I'll throw them off of my land and starve their wives and children. Those men who bled the ground red at Falkirk fought for William Wallace. He fights for something that I never had. And I took it from him when I betrayed him. I saw it in his face on the battlefield, and it's tearing me apart."

He stands there looking as if he's just sold his soul. His father, trying to somehow reassure his son, says, "All men betray. All men lose heart."

"I don't want to lose heart!" Robert shouts, rivers of tears flowing down his face. "I want to believe as he does."

For me it's perhaps the most powerful moment in this classic movie. There's something about young Bruce's bitter words of remorse that hit me deeply. I empathize with his words because I know I've lost heart at times in my life. I desperately want to believe rather than betray.

Luke 18:1 says, "Then He spoke a parable to them, that men always ought to pray and not lose heart" (NKJV, emphasis mine).

The Greek word used here for "lose heart" is egkakeo, which means "become discouraged, to lose courage, to be weary in anything, flag, faint."

Paul the apostle also uses this word in his letters to the Corinthians (2 Corinthians 4:1, 16), Galatians (6:9), Ephesians (3:13), and Thessalonians (2 Thessalonians 3:13).

It's tempting to throw in the towel when we don't see the answer to our prayer that we want. In a world that grinds us down, it would be much easier simply to forfeit the match rather than show up and fight. The tempter is there at every pivotal moment whispering those poisonous words, "All men betray. All men lose heart."

But our great Champion, who smashed the head of that slimy serpent, calls us to follow him onto the battlefield. To persist in prayer, burn with belief, and fight in faith.

And one day, like William Wallace, we'll let out a primal cry in the face of our enemy: "Freedom!"

Reflection: In what ways have you found yourself empathizing with Robert the Bruce? What is it that Jesus is calling you to resume fighting for in prayer?

CONCLUSION

Over the last twenty-one days, we've barely scratched the surface when it comes to the many encounters with Jesus found in the four Gospels written by Matthew, Mark, Luke, and John. In fact, John finishes his Gospel account with these words: "Jesus also did many other things. If they were all written down, I suppose the whole world could not contain the books that would be written" (John 21:25).

Since John wrote those words nearly two thousand years ago, this same Jesus has encountered billions of people like you and me all over the world. Like John, we can move beyond an initial encounter and into a long-term embrace.

Every religion on earth except Christianity is mankind's attempt at reaching God. With Christianity, God reached down to mankind through Jesus. Any love we experience is because God first loved us (1 John 4:19).

Jesus is the "author and finisher of our faith," and we have the wonderful privilege of being characters in the grand story he's continuing to write (Hebrews 12:2 NKJV).

How about you? Are you trusting Jesus as your only hope beyond the grave? Listen to these clear words spoken by the Master himself: "I tell you the truth, those who listen to my message and believe in God who sent me have eternal life. They will never be condemned for their sins, but they have already passed from death into life" (John 5:24).

When we believe something, we're putting our full weight into it. Like the "trust fall" game you may have played, we're falling into the arms of Jesus, trusting he'll catch us. It's a complete surrender to the One who paid for our sin when he hung on a cruel Roman cross.

The "beloved disciple," John, adds even more clarity with these simple words: "Whoever has the Son has life; whoever does not have God's Son does not have life" (1 John 5:12).

If you have any doubts concerning your eternity, those doubts can be removed today. It's as simple as taking this first step: "Everyone who calls on the name of the LORD will be saved" (Romans 10:13).

You can call on the name of Jesus using a prayer something like this:

Jesus, I confess my need for the salvation found in you alone. I'm tired of living life on my own terms. I invite you to take up residence in my life. I surrender to your will for my life. I lay all of my sins, including my idols and addictions, at the foot of the cross you died upon. Change me from the inside out and give me new desires that please you. Break my heart with the things that break yours. Stamp eternity upon my eyes. Help me to live for you each new day. Thank you for your grace and mercy toward me. It's in Jesus's name I pray, amen.

Now, I want to encourage you to continue growing in your faith by taking the following steps:

1. Read the Bible (God's Word) each day. This is like daily soul food as we partake of the buffet God has offered us. I personally enjoy reading a chapter from the New Testament and Old Testament to begin each day. As Hebrews 4:12 says, "For the word of God is alive and powerful. It is sharper than the sharpest two-edged sword, cutting between soul and spirit, between joint and marrow. It exposes our innermost thoughts and desires."

2. Connect to a local church. It's important to meet with a local body of believers on a regular basis in order both to receive and to give encourage-

ment. Find a solid Bible-believing church where the pastor teaches from the Bible. We need other Christian brothers and sisters in our lives. As Proverbs 27:17 says, "As iron sharpens iron, so a friend sharpens a friend."

3. Commit to regular prayer. You and I now have direct access to the Father through Jesus. Prayer is simply "talkin' with Daddy." Morning, afternoon, evening, or night. There's no bad time to spend time in prayer. What a joy to have 24/7 access to the God of the universe. It's about intimate relationship. One of my favorite verses in Scripture is Psalm 27:8, which says, "My heart has heard you say, 'Come and talk with me.' And my heart responds, 'LORD, I am coming.'"

Here's to many more wonderful encounters with Jesus!

ABOUT CJ HITZ

CJ Hitz and his wife, Shelley, enjoy sharing God's Truth through their speaking engagements and their writing. They enjoy spending time outdoors running, hiking, and exploring God's beautiful creation. CJ and Shelley reside in Colorado Springs, Colorado.

To find out more about CJ and to contact him about speaking at your next event in person or online, send an email to cj@cjhitz.com or find him at www.body-andsoulpublishing.com/about-cj-hitz.

Note from the Author: Reviews are gold to authors! If you have enjoyed this book, would you consider reviewing it on Amazon.com? Thank you!